Book of Life
SELF DISCOVERY

Re-written my story — A New Canvas of my Life from Self Discovery to Self Worth... The Road Less Travelled - Filet to a Cream

LAKSHIT ROHIT KOTHARI

Qurate
quratebooks.com

Book of Life - Self Discovery
Lakshit Rohit Kothari

Published in 2025

© Published by

Qurate Books Pvt. Ltd.
Goa 403523, India
www.quratebooks.com
Tel: 1800-210-6527, Email: info@quratebooks.com

ISBN: 978-93-58985-99-3

Contents

Chapter 1

The Office & The Computer

My earliest memories of learning carry a strange duality. I was a child visiting my father's office, meant to study but drawn instead to the computer—the cricket games I played with Kishore bhai, my father's colleague, were my real lessons. My father had his own way of teaching. He would only show me the first and last pages of a book. He said it was "funny," but I later understood it as a metaphor for life: the first and last pages are written for us—birth and death—while the middle pages are ours to fill.

That idea stayed with me. I became an observer. I watched life unfold and questioned the reflections

I saw. At times, I felt lonely, weighed down by comparisons and a quiet sense of victimhood. Others seemed to have it easier. But slowly a shift began. I began to see purpose in the struggle. Making the world better wasn't just a grand idea; it was a personal journey of growth and discovery.

I wanted to break free—from the limits I had set for myself, from the conditions and norms handed to me. I wanted to build my own world, defined by my values. I learned to love myself, also to rely on my own strength, and to admire those who had faced adversity and still chased their dreams.

Naruto became my hero. He carried loneliness and rejection like a second skin, trained relentlessly, and never gave up. From him I learned perseverance and the power of self-reliance. Shikamaru taught me that the next generation is everything. The question is always the same: what can we do today so the children of tomorrow live and learn better?

Books like *Atomic Habits* showed me how to shape change. Cue, craving, response, reward—four laws to build good habits and break the bad. I learned to forgive myself for past missteps and the years

I lived by society's expectations. I began to trust that everything I seek is already mine by grace.

I am grateful—for the chance to work at Tiger, for the lessons hidden in each challenge, for the people whose quiet teachings shaped me. Even small steps, like contributing to a Milaap crowd funding campaign, felt like a beginning. I ask myself: How can I make change obvious, attractive, easy, satisfying? By living authentically and taking responsibility for my actions.

I have faced my own contradictions. I once promised to quit smoking but didn't. I relied on small external comforts for short-term satisfaction. I grew up privileged, yet privilege never shielded me from struggle. Others may envy what they think I have, but peace is earned, not given.

I no longer judge. Everyone carries their own private battles. My faith is in God and in the actions I take. I live by the vision I see for myself. I know now that to grow, I must move with time, accept criticism, and celebrate progress—even when it hurts.

I have mentors and angels, even if they never wore the title: Akansha, who nourishes my thoughts; my father, who trusted me to drive both on the highway and in life; friends and colleagues whose presence teaches more than words. Even my elder brother taught me a lot of things, same goes my mother, as well. My grandmother one who passed away years ago has always stayed by my side.

Meditation grounds me. The Beej mantras—Lam, Vam, Ram, Yam, Hum, Om, Aum—tune me to something larger. *Aham Brahmasmi*—I am the universe. *Neti Neti*—I am not this body, not these thoughts, not these emotions. Slowly, I have unnumbed myself. I have stopped letting others steer my life. I have left behind the people-pleasing, the old beliefs, the fear.

The corporate chapter nears its end, and I feel no regret. This is a fresh start. I want to create, to work with technology and art, to build games and animate worlds. I see myself as an entrepreneur, a valuepreneur, a G.O.A.T in my industry by January 19, 2027. I want to stand beside other creative, visionary people and build something larger than life.

I have learned to rely on myself. To heal without announcing my wounds. To accept that every hard night and lonely hour has prepared me for what comes next. My faith is in action over reaction, in silence and pause for guidance. I know I am stronger than I once believed, and I understand now that I am here not to work off karma but to fulfill my dharma.

This is my Nataraja's dance—a dance of valor disguised as struggle. I move forward with gratitude, with the knowledge that I carry every tool I need within me. The old self no longer belongs here. I am ready to write the middle pages of my book—and this time, they will be mine.

Chapter 2

"Nothing Last Forever"

Shiva's Dance of Valor opens the portal to live through the Trials and Tribulation of life which brings our love back when given externally too much willed through it where we have lost our Valor of life, love and perseverance to create better life by destroying the old. The life taught by It is very easy to sway things way when finding no ground to emotional balance, or to hold on the very plaintive sense of life. To what the see now has more change then ever and many areas it has been the way how so many were able to hold there ground to know how strong they can grow with every step by step each minute it is a test. To grow spiritually profound.

What it seems like every anime watched had a different style of telling a meaning. Every challenge had a purpose. Inazuma Eleven an anime a character name Endou Mamoru who played as a goal keeper. He always smiled, in every challenge and stood up against the most dangerous of people and even against his own friends. Because he had a purpose of building his grandfathers dream, to reborn the love of his football team to take part in National Level Football Game. His team won, the nationals in Japan. With every grit and hardship but what advanced them ahead was the team work. The team work was inspiring. What it meant was that if one falls down the whole team went down, if even one inspired the other stands up and then whole team stood. Even if it makes them to slip through some of the most notorious line of action they took that helped them to move ahead. Because in life every thing does not work straight.

Every path has to be taken in waves. There is no right path it's a maze walk in a loop without knowing, what's the purpose we keep walking or running, then a question raises should we follow the crowd and keep moving in the life direction without any penance or Can we/should we walk on our own path, that can help us grow with those who have learnt to grow by taking measures and follow through, step by step with no preferential cause where the need of an hour happens only when it is needed but also happens without any need, but to fulfill the deed.

There are a lot of positive change happened when I started to work on me after I let go the control of controlling myself to stay in the same space in 2024 when my power domain of Ajna chakra (Third Eye Chakra) Opened. Now that I have let myself free it's time for me to grow and become the version that I really love to see myself as.

I have learnt to respect myself more. There were some more people in my life who taught me a lot of thing stayed with me for sometime been good friends and one so called my Ex who stayed with me for short time went away and I had fallen, knew no strength to have her, how to lift myself as I was told by my own people I have no Status in the society why would she become yours. But they who went away those who rejected me brought new things in life and light that changed my perspective in life.

So, many times in my childhood as well I never had anyone good in my life because I had no status, I lived that pain and stayed in fear, I felt ashamed. For that reason I had gotten into addiction of something that kept me stayed stuck in fear and kept bringing the same analogy of life that I have lived I was not able to free myself from that. I had somehow learnt to accept my loneliness, and let others control my life. With no regrets I can say I have been an insecure person with Hidden Red Flag nature Psychologically.

This is the thing of the yesterday on my life there is nothing I could do, until life taught me how I can be what I can become, now, without regret. I change when I change my story my life my world of past.

This metaphor feels right it was illusion of my past and the conditioning that left me stay in defeated stature and made me stay in the aura . I learnt to forgive myself, forgive my heart, why did I let myself live like a downtrodden. I also, got chance to change everything but I kept rejecting it because I wanted people to teach me. Give me importance as well but that only made me rely on others instead. The past self the past aura that itself never wanted to last for ever. Just as the chapter says "NOTHING LASTS FOREVER".

That what people say. Then it is time that I don't sit in the same side of life. It's time to make a move. It's time to move past the norms of life and grow without fear. Breaking all odds. As, I understand, I see, I speak, I love I feel, I do, I am already a G.O.A.T. I Lakshit Kothari release myself from the past karmic cords with self and everyone else. Here in this life I have come to become Lakshit and co. Self Love for every other nature of mine. Only to accept rise and know no bounds to held back.

Chapter 3

An Era of Respect — The Photographer's Journey

In the lanes of Vadodara, among temples, palaces, and the hum of everyday life, there was once a boy known in his father's community not for business, not for politics, but for the way he *saw*. He wasn't just looking at the world—he was framing it, catching light, shadows, and silence in a way others could never quite manage.

People still ask me today: *"Are you still a photographer?" Are still working as a Photographer?*

I smile, sometimes with a hint of ache, and reply, *"Not the way I used to be."* Because there was a time when the camera wasn't just a tool—it was my heartbeat.

I had the honor of learning under **Rahul Gajjar**, the renowned storyteller of Vadodara's soul, a master with the lens. His studio, *Raaga Numerique*, was not just a workspace, it was a temple of vision. Rahul sir took the stones of Champaner, the majestic expanse of Pavagadh, the grandeur of Laxmi Vilas Palace, and turned them into living poetry. Under his guidance, I walked through exhibitions, joined photography walks, and even transformed ancient motifs into jewelry designs. I wasn't just learning photography—I was learning how to narrate history without words. I learned what is the game of life, he was the first guru who really loved me better then those who have been part of my life.

There came a day when one of my photographs stood tall in an exhibition by SOCLEEN Vadodara, and VNM News interviewed me. For a fleeting moment, it felt like the city itself had paused to watch through my eyes. That was the era when I understood respect—not as applause, but as being seen.

But life, as it does, shifted. My body wasn't always strong enough to stand through long hours behind the lens. That chapter had to rest. I told myself: *"What's gone is gone."* Yet deep inside, I knew—chapters don't die, they just wait for the right moment to return in a new form.

And so I wandered. From photography, I flowed into videography, films, 3D design, modeling, animation—every corner of the creative field I could touch. I stumbled, made mistakes, took wrong turns, and at times, failed to grow because I didn't yet understand how money, clients, and negotiation worked. But each wrong choice carved me into someone sturdier, more self-aware.

I shot industrial stills for Rhino Machine Foundry, where my photographs still hang in their space. I captured products for the company I work with today, stretching my creativity in ways that prove—once a photographer, always a photographer.

Because photography is not about holding a camera—it's about capturing a vision. It's about seeing the extraordinary in the ordinary. And as the saying goes:

“A creative visual expressed through any medium tells a story that is never forgotten.”

Chapter 4

Filet to a Cream

In a quiet village, there once lived a blacksmith.

He was famed across the land for his craft. His swords never bent, his knives never dulled. Travelers came from distant places to own his creations, for each blade was a triumph of discipline—steel stripped of excess, shaped into pure essence. His hands knew the rhythm of fire and hammer, and his heart beat to the tune of precision.

One evening, as the forge glowed with dying embers, an old monk wandered into the blacksmith's shop. But he asked not for a sword. Instead, he asked for a cup of milk. Surprised, the blacksmith poured one for him. The monk sat silently, sipping until the cream slowly rose to the surface.

Setting the cup down, the monk spoke:

"Do you see how the cream rises? A blade survives by cutting, but cream survives by softening. One endures through sharpness, the other through richness. Tell me, blacksmith—do you wish to cut, or do you wish to rise?"

The words struck harder than any hammer against iron. All his life, the blacksmith had been the filet—sharp, disciplined, unyielding. His craft was survival, his edge his identity. Yet something within him longed for more. He yearned not just to endure, but to transcend.

The monk left. But his question remained.

◇ My Reflection

I am that blacksmith.

Once, I was the filet—honed by struggle, precise and unbending. Filet is discipline. It is survival. It is the blade that stands firm in the fire of life. For years, it carried me forward. But filet alone is not fullness. Filet is essence, yes, but it is rigid. It cuts, yet it cannot flow.

And so I spoke to my universe: *Transform me. Do not let me remain only a blade. Melt me. Sweeten me. Make me whole.*

The alchemy began. The sharp edge softened. Refinement gave way to richness. The survivor learned to rise.

From filet, I became cream.

Cream is not weakness–it is the most precious part. It holds abundance, softness, nourishment, and luxury. It flows where the blade cannot. It rises above, not by fighting, but by surrendering to its true nature.

This is the path of my spirit:

- From raw edge to rare glow.
- From discipline to abundance.
- From filet to cream.

◇ My Declaration

I did not lose myself in softening–I expanded myself.

Filet gave me strength. Cream gave me surrender. Filet taught me to cut away what does not belong. Cream taught me to rise above, carrying sweetness with me. Together, they form my wholeness.

So I declare to the universe and to myself:

I am Filet to a Cream.

The warrior who became the poet, the blade that learned to flow, the survivor who chose to rise. This is not just a phrase. It is my creed. My command. My offering.

Chapter 5

Leaders Eat Last

The first book I read in 2023 was *Leaders Eat Last* by Simon Sinek, introduced to me by my friend Ashutosh in Mumbai. To be frank, this book opened my eyes to the true essence of leadership—the way authority, vision, and information must all come together. I realized that when a leader has authority and information but lacks vision, flaws will always exist in the system. Whether as a professional or as a company owner, such a leader is bound to fail. A leader who cannot lead by example, no matter how many clients he secures or how strong a workforce he gathers, will eventually fall short if he does not create better systems, planning, and strategy. Without that, even the most talented people are reduced to working like donkeys—stripped of respect, purpose, and creativity.

Leadership, I came to understand, is not about position or power. It is a choice. A true leader builds a company by sharing vision with the team—not just to be visionary, but to bring out the best in every person's potential, instead of discarding it like something worthless. Leadership means challenging both self and team to let go of old, stagnant ways of working, and to rise together into a new norm. When a leader grows, the team must grow too. Even in a startup, the leader who earns trust by aligning talented people with a clear vision is far more likely to win than one who does not.

I once saw how this played out in a company buzzing with deadlines and competition. The atmosphere was tense, each person guarding their own corner, shoulders heavy with the burden of constant comparison. Then came a leader who quietly shifted everything—not through orders barked across the room, but through the simple act of putting people first. He listened when others spoke. He shielded his team from unnecessary stress. He built what Simon Sinek would call a *Circle of Safety*.

Inside that circle, trust began to bloom. People stopped glancing over their shoulders and instead leaned into each other's strengths. The old cocktail of cortisol and fear drained away, replaced by the chemistry of belonging—serotonin and oxytocin flowing as freely as laughter in late-night brainstorming sessions. Achievements no longer felt like solitary victories but shared milestones, each success sparking dopamine and endorphins without leaving anyone behind.

One day, the team faced a project so risky it threatened to undo months of progress. Rather than demanding perfection, their leader stepped forward, absorbing the weight of responsibility so his people wouldn't have to. Like Johnny Bravo, the pilot who once dove into enemy fire to protect his men, this leader stood in the line of blame, shielding his team from criticism so they could focus fully on the mission. It wasn't grand speeches or the exercise of authority that inspired them—it was sacrifice, quiet and deliberate.

By the time the project launched, no one doubted the direction they were heading. They worked not out of fear of failure, but from trust in each other and in the one who led them. Within that circle of safety, creativity thrived. Together, they achieved far more than they ever could alone.

In the end, the story wasn't about power or position. It was about service—the leader who ate last so his people could rise first.

ꕥ☆ꕥ

Chapter 6

The Seeds of Change

Before I discovered the quiet power of Atomic Habits, life felt like a tangled mess of routines that didn't belong to me. My days were strung together by habits of fear, failure, regret, and a desperate need to feel safe by leaning on the comfort of others. I lived by the conditions others set for me, drifting wherever their expectations carried me. The irony was sharp—I craved change, yet clung so tightly to the past that even when change knocked on my door, I ran back to the same people, the same patterns, the same old life that suffocated me.

It was a cycle of replay. Over and over again, I found myself acting out the same story, as if my life was stuck on loop. I thought safety lived in repetition, but all it brought was stagnation. The truth was harsh but undeniable: new beginnings cannot bloom when your hands are still gripping the weeds of yesterday.

The turning point came not with a thunderclap of revelation, but in whispers—lessons I learned from people around me who didn't even know they were teaching. Some spoke through their actions, some through their resilience, and some through their quiet persistence. I began to notice a pattern: the ones who grew, the ones who thrived, had built their lives around habits that lifted them higher, not dragged them back.

Then came James Clear's words in *Atomic Habits*—a mirror to my soul: **"Every action you take is a vote for the type of person you wish to become. No single instance will transform your beliefs, but as the votes build up, so does the evidence of your new identity."**

That struck me. I realized my life wasn't built in grand decisions or sudden transformations. It was built in the tiniest of choices, the ones I thought were invisible. The way I reacted to a problem.

The way I treated my mornings. The way I chose to eat, move, speak, rest. Each one was a vote. And all my votes had been for the wrong candidate—fear, regret, stagnation. No wonder my life felt rigged.

Change, I discovered, isn't magic. It's math. You don't snap your fingers and wake up as someone new. You evolve—bit by bit, day by day, habit by habit. James Clear calls it "microevolutions of the self." The phrase stayed with me, reminding me that even the smallest step counts, because steps add up.

I remember the story of his friend who lost over 100 pounds. Her secret? A simple question: *What would a healthy person do?* She asked it every day, in every decision. Would a healthy person take the cab or walk? Would a healthy person order a burrito or a salad? With each answer, she cast a vote for her new identity. Slowly, her body and her life transformed.

That became my compass too. *What would a stronger person do? What would a kinder person do? What would a braver person do?* The answers didn't always come easy, but when I followed them, the path ahead began to change.

And the method was clear: four laws of habit formation, like stepping stones across a river.

1. **Make it obvious** – I stopped hiding my new habits in the shadows. If I wanted to read more, I left books in plain sight. If I wanted to exercise, I placed my shoes by the door. My environment began to vote with me.

2. **Make it attractive** – I tied habits to rewards. A long walk became an excuse to listen to my favorite podcast. Writing each morning felt less like a chore when paired with the ritual of coffee. The process became something I looked forward to.

3. **Make it easy** – I stopped chasing perfection. Tiny steps mattered. Two push-ups were better than none. Writing a single paragraph was better than waiting for inspiration to write ten pages. I lowered the barrier to entry and suddenly, consistency was possible.

4. **Make it satisfying** – I celebrated the small wins. Each day I stuck with a new habit, I let myself feel the victory. I didn't wait for the "big moment" of success. Progress itself became its own reward.

Slowly, life shifted. Not dramatically at first—just quietly, steadily. The mess didn't vanish overnight, but it began to take shape. Like sculpting stone, the chips fell away bit by bit, revealing the form beneath. Each tiny change became a seed, and over time, those seeds grew roots. Roots strong enough to hold me, habits strong enough to guide me.

The life I live now is not an accident. It's a garden I chose to plant. And the lesson is simple but profound: if you want to change your life, change your habits. If you want to change your habits, start small. One vote, one step, one seed at a time.

Chapter 7

Marathon — Running the Marathon of Life

In 2024, I began running marathons. At first, it was simply a challenge, a chance I took on something I had never thought I'd do. By 2025, running had transformed me. It helped me refocus, rebuild, and rediscover myself. The more I worked on my physique and health, the more I found a deeper truth: I had begun to love myself.

I wasn't alone in this journey. I had a trainer who guided me with discipline and patience. Meditation became a part of my routine, and with it, the heavy aura of fear I once carried slowly lifted away. At the CEAT Marathon and later the Vadodara Marathon, I didn't have friends or family in the audience cheering me on. But there was one voice that never left me—that of my own. And for that, I am grateful.

Living in Mumbai had taught me how to push myself physically, but when I moved back under my father's roof, I doubted whether I could continue. It felt too easy to slip into comfort. Yet zeal proved stronger than comfort. I ran the CEAT Marathon in Vadodara, finishing the 10 km race in 1 hour and 2 minutes—a result that changed my life. Soon after, under the training of Tapash Deo Sir, I grew hungrier, more energized, more determined. Injuries tested me, but guidance from healers at 360 Physiotherapy, along with support from Sumit Sir, Jahnvi Joshi, Puja, and others, helped me recover and grow.

The Vadodara Marathon followed, and I completed it in 1 hour and 10 minutes. That morning, I still remember the smell of sweat and damp earth as runners gathered at the start line. The cool air buzzed with nerves and excitement. When the horn sounded, thousands of footsteps thundered across the road in unison, like a giant heartbeat shaking the ground. I wasn't racing against them. I was only racing against myself. The cheers of strangers blended with the pounding in my chest, and in that noise, I found silence—my own inner voice telling me to keep going. Crossing the finish line, surrounded by more than 5,000 people, I realized the race wasn't about winning. It was about becoming.

The atmosphere of a marathon is electric, almost spiritual. It strips you down, makes you face yourself, and then gifts you back a stronger version of who you are. For me, the universe's greatest gift was learning not to lean on comfort, but to chase growth.

I once applied for the Mumbai Marathon, hoping to fulfill my dream of running the 42 km dream run. When I was rejected, I cried. Not because of failure, but because I knew the sweat, the discipline, and the countless hours I had poured into that dream. That rejection didn't end my dream—it only reminded me how much it mattered to me. I still carry that dream, and beyond it, the vision of completing a triathlon.

Running has taught me that healing is not just about physical strength. It's about mindset, mentality, and spirituality. Each step is both a cure and a creation. The rhythm of footsteps, the burn in the muscles, the quiet conversations with myself—all of it is part of the journey. And so, I remind myself: Lakshit Kothari, you are remaking yourself. *Aham Brahmasmi.* "Every step I run reminds me: Aham Brahmasmi—I am the universe, limitless, enduring, and enough, I will keep running..."

Chapter 8

Freelancing — From Failure to Success

I walked into freelancing like a bright-eyed traveler without a map—ambition in my pocket, talent on my tongue, and no clue about the terrain ahead. At first, everything felt possible. Soon enough, every client email, every contract clause, every missed deadline taught me the truth: talent will open a door, but it won't keep you standing in the corridor. Freelancing demanded something else—discipline, systems, clarity of purpose, and the stubborn business of showing up.

Opportunities arrived like seasonal winds. Some warmed my face and disappeared. Some carried me forward. One offer from France—still—sits at the back of my throat as a regret, a could-have-been that tastes like cold coffee. Even in failure, though, the universe kept whispering: I will keep sending what you ask for, but will you rise to receive it?

That question pierced me in quiet moments. Was I willing to lift myself?

I started to study myself the way I used to study references—frame by frame. Mistake after mistake revealed a pattern: fear dressing up as caution, old stories steering my choices, and the habit of calling myself a generalist when I didn't know what I was selling. Awareness became the first tool I learned to use. With it, I began carving new ground.

It's strange how guidance appears when you are both humble and hungry. For the first time in a long while, I stopped pretending I had to do it alone. I found mentors, people who nudged and corrected without drama. I felt something steadier than advice—the presence of the gods I grew up with, an inner force that felt like Lord Shiva and Goddess Shakti reminding me of my spine: stand, breathe, act. With that quiet faith, I walked in faith, not fear.

Then last Saturday, a meeting cut cleanly through the fog.

Roman Pillai from **Kupa Creative** sat across from me—not an interview, not a sermon, just a conversation about character animation that gently expanded into the whole messy ecosystem of freelancing, AR/VR, and the balance between craft and cash. We began with rigs and timing, and finished in strategy. He told me Krupa had flirted with AR but that their heartbeat right now was character animation—deep, focused, collaborative work done with seasoned pros. Their approach wasn't flashy; it was deliberate. It reminded me of studios that fold AR into the pipeline slowly, like Triumph Design Studio: a marathon of integration, not a sprint.

When we stepped back and looked at the market, a pattern shone through: **3D character animation is on fire.** Brands want personality. Agencies want believable motion. Indie creators want characters that carry stories. Video editing remains vital—especially for social content—but it often pairs best with automation and AI: a bridge, not the destination.

That was the moment I felt the hinge inside me click. My path couldn't be about chasing every tool or collecting every gig like shiny stones. It had to be about story and soul—making short films with heart while building a portfolio that spoke clearer than any elevator pitch.

Then came the awkward truth. Roman asked me about my work, and I did not meet him the way I should have. My portfolio wasn't ready; my words swelled to cover gaps; I stretched truths where truth would have served me better. I left the meeting knowing I'd deflated trust. He said he'd check with his co-founder. There may be a second meeting. There may not. Either way, the mirror had been held up.

I didn't hide behind excuses. I taught him a few technical shortcuts—iClone, Mixamo, Auto Rig—because they do the heavy lifting for character work, speed up pipelines, and let you focus on acting and intention. But teaching tools was not the same as owning a craft.

I realized then: I cannot be a 3D generalist forever. The market punishes fuzzy positioning. The freelancers who succeed know exactly what they sell and to whom. They show up with a sharp edge and a clear voice. So I made a choice.

I would double down on character animation—not as a checklist of software skills, but as an actor-director-tool kitted discipline. I would study acting for animators. I would refine timing, weight, micro-expressions, and emotional arcs until a short loop could land a gut-punch. I would design smarter workflows, adopt better tools, and keep the humility to stay a student.

Two opportunities sat on my table: steady work with steady pay, and the riskier, lonelier path of deeper freelancing. Each had lessons. Why choose only one when both could train me? I decided to learn from both—use stable gigs to pay rent while my riskier investments sharpened my edge.

That meeting with Roman did more than open a possibility; it exposed where I stumbled and where I stood tall. It taught me the hardest lesson: in freelancing, honesty is a skill. Bring your truth. If your portfolio is thin, say so. If your acting chops need practice, say so. But never arrive with an incomplete picture masquerading as finished work.

So I rewrote my plan. I would become a solopreneur with a niche: characters that behave like people. My tools—iClone, Mixamo, Auto Rig—would be servants of my craft, not its master. I would learn to sell not by volume, but by the clarity of what I deliver: believable, acting-driven character animation.

The industry is changing. Machines will remove grunt work; studios will standardize pipelines; clients will ask for more personality in less time. That change is grace if you are ready for it. It's also an invitation: sharpen, choose, and show up.

When the curtain rises again on this life, I will make it a performance worth remembering. No more fuzzy labels. No more hiding. I will show up with the truth of my work shining on the screen—and, finally, with the confidence to let it speak for me.

Chapter 9

Valuepreneur

There was once a kind of entrepreneur who wasn't obsessed with the chase for money, the race for status, or the applause of quick wins. This person was different. They weren't building just a business; they were building something far more precious—value. People began to call them *Valuepreneur*.

A Valuepreneur wakes each morning with a simple question: *"Whose life will I make better today?"* That question becomes the compass, pointing them toward customers, communities, and futures yet unseen.

The Principles They Live By

At the heart of every Valuepreneur beats customer-centricity. They don't sit behind walls of assumption; they listen. They ask. They adapt. Products, services, and ideas become mirrors reflecting what people truly need.

Their second pillar is impact. For them, business is not just transactions, it's transformation. A Valuepreneur plants seeds of change—sometimes small, sometimes mighty—that ripple through families, societies, even generations.

And while many chase short-term sparks, a Valuepreneur sees the horizon. Their long-term vision stretches beyond profit sheets, reaching for legacies that endure. Along that journey, they walk with integrity, guided by ethical practices. Transparency is not a strategy; it is their nature.

Stories of Value-driven Entrepreneurs

Anaya the Baker

In a small town lived Anaya, a young woman who opened a bakery. At first glance, it was like any other—bread, cakes, and the smell of sugar in the air. But Anaya wasn't just selling pastries;

she was creating something more. She noticed the farmers struggling to sell their grain at fair prices, so she sourced directly from them. She asked her customers about their childhood flavours and brought those memories to life in her recipes.

Her shop became a gathering place, a community hub where stories were shared over warm loaves. Years later, when larger chains tried to muscle into her market, the town stood by her side. They weren't loyal to a bakery; they were loyal to *her*, because she had been loyal to them all along.

Ravi the Coder

In a buzzing city, Ravi built a small tech Start-up. He could have gone the usual route—chasing venture capital, scaling fast, selling data. But Ravi had a different compass. He built software for small, local shops who couldn't afford the fancy digital tools big corporations used. His apps were simple, affordable, and designed with empathy. He spent weekends in shop fronts, listening to owners explain their challenges.

Instead of becoming just another tech company, Ravi became a quiet enabler of livelihoods. Street vendors could track sales, tailors could manage orders, and grocers could finally compete with supermarkets. His profits grew, yes, but his impact grew wider. He wasn't just coding; he was levelling the playing field.

Meera the Designer

Meera started as a freelance graphic designer. She loved aesthetics, but what truly drove her was storytelling. Instead of just making logos, she sat with small non-profits, listening to their missions. She created visual identities that didn't just look pretty but *spoke powerfully*. For a women's collective, she designed packaging that celebrated traditional patterns and brought dignity to their craft. For an environmental group, she built campaigns that mobilized thousands.

Her work wasn't the most lucrative at first, but it carried soul. Over time, her reputation grew—not just as a designer but as someone who gave movements their voice. Clients didn't just hire her; they trusted her with their dreams.

Arjun the Dream Architect

In the near future, Arjun was building worlds—not with bricks, but with pixels and code. An AR/VR creator, he could have spent his days designing games for quick profit. Instead, he chose a different path. Arjun created immersive classrooms for children in rural villages, where history wasn't read from books but *lived*—students could walk through ancient civilizations, swim with sea creatures, or stand on Mars.

He partnered with teachers, non-profits, and local leaders to make education not just accessible but unforgettable. Investors pushed him to commercialize aggressively, but Arjun held his ground. His vision was clear: technology should amplify human potential, not just entertain. Over time, his platform became a global movement in education, giving millions of children experiences their parents never dreamed possible.

Arjun didn't just design realities—he expanded them.

The Thread That Connects Them

From Anaya's warm bakery to Ravi's quiet coding desk, from Meera's sketches to Arjun's digital worlds, one truth ties them all together: value comes before profit, and purpose comes before pride. Each of them shows that industries may differ, tools may evolve, and times may change, but the heart of a Valuepreneur remains constant.

They listen. They care. They build. They give. And in return, they gain something no balance sheet can measure: trust, love, and legacy.

The Rewards of Walking This Path

The path of the Valuepreneur isn't always easy, but it is rich. There is fulfilment in knowing your work leaves more than numbers–it leaves meaning. Customers, sensing authenticity, give back with fierce loyalty. A reputation, once earned for honesty and care, becomes a shield that protects and uplifts. And with value as the foundation, growth becomes sustainable, not fragile.

In Essence

A Valuepreneur is more than a businessperson. They are a storyteller, a bridge-builder, a quiet revolutionary. They stand as proof that business can be more than a mechanism for wealth–it can be a force for good, a tool for change, a vessel for hope.

To be a Valuepreneur is to believe that the true profit of business lies not in what we take, but in what we give back.

It is a journey where success is measured not by the heights of financial peaks but by the depths of human connection and the breadth of positive impact. In a world often driven by competition and haste, the Valuepreneur stands as a beacon of what is possible when empathy and action converge.

As more people embrace this path, a new narrative unfolds—one where businesses are ecosystems of collaboration and compassion, where success stories are written not in dollars, but in lives touched. This is not just an ideal; it is a movement, a call to all who dare to dream beyond the conventional.

And so, the legacy of the Valuepreneur grows, inspiring a generation to lift others as they climb, to innovate with heart, and to transform industries with kindness. In their hands, business is not just a series of transactions, but a tapestry of stories woven with purpose and promise.

The world awaits more Valuepreneur, ready to write the chapters of tomorrow with courage and hope. Will you join them?

Chapter 10

The Dial of the Mind

I never thought of my mind as a radio until the day I stumbled across José Silva's method. To me, thoughts were just noise—loud, restless, often cruel. Growing up, life didn't hand me silver spoons. Bills haunted the table. Opportunities slipped through fingers that were always reaching but rarely grasping. I wanted peace. I wanted control. And for a long time, I thought both were for people richer, luckier, smarter than me.

Then one evening, curiosity cracked something open. I sat still, closed my eyes, tilted them upward, and whispered the countdown Silva taught: "3...3...3. 2...2...2. 1...1...1." By the time I reached the silent descent from 50, the chaos had thinned. For the first time in years, the static softened into silence. Not sleep. Not escape. Something better. It felt like steering, not drifting.

I imagined a screen in my mind. At first, it was blurry, flickering. Then clear: I saw myself confident, unshaken, building a life of abundance. I whispered, *I'm capable. I'm calm. I will make this real.* When I counted back up and opened my eyes, nothing outside had changed—the room was still dim, the bills still there. But inside, I felt different. Stronger. Aligned.

Night after night, I returned. The 3-2-1 became my doorway. The Mirror of the Mind became my canvas. I practiced Silva's tricks: the Three-Finger Technique to summon calm before big moments, the Glass-of-Water trick when I needed answers, Dream Control to turn my nights into laboratories of intuition. Each practice carved out space inside me where fear once lived.

Slowly, the external world bent to the internal shift. My work sharpened. My creativity expanded. Ideas found me instead of me chasing them. The boy who once worried about every rupee grew into a man running businesses, hiring others, and shaping his own economy. Scarcity faded into sufficiency, then into abundance.

Success came—but it did not intoxicate me. Because every time I entered alpha, every time I slowed into that quiet, I saw more than myself. I saw children like me, hungry for chances. I saw families chasing light in the dark. I whispered different affirmations now: *I use my wealth to lift others. My success is their seed too.*

And so, when abundance turned into wealth, and wealth turned into more than enough, I turned outward. Schools, programs, opportunities for others—they became the true treasures. A billionaire, yes. But a philanthropist, more importantly. Because peace and satisfaction never came from numbers in a bank—they came from seeing lives lifted by the overflow of my own journey.

Today, when people ask me what self-discovery means, I tell them this: it's not about finding yourself once and for all. It's about learning to tune the dial of your mind. Beta will always be there—the noise, the chaos. But alpha? That's where you program peace. That's where you build vision. That's where you create a life worth living, not just for you, but for everyone your life touches.

The Silva Method gave me that dial. And I chose to turn it.

Reflection for Readers: Close your eyes tonight. Breathe. Count 3-2-1. Step into your own alpha. Don't just dream—program. Don't just wish—affirm. Imagine the life you want, then anchor it. Because if a poor boy like me can retune his mind, build abundance, and share it with the world, so can you.

ཐ☆ཐ

Chapter 11

The Second Brain — From Chaos to Clarity

There was a time my mind felt like a crowded marketplace. Thoughts clashed like vendors shouting over one another. Ideas came in bright flashes—too many to hold, too slippery to trust. Some would vanish before I could write them down. Others would sit heavy in notebooks, never to be seen again.

It wasn't that I lacked creativity. In fact, creativity was my abundance. What I lacked was a **system**—a way to honor the flood of thoughts and turn them into something lasting.

Then came Tiago Forte's *Building a Second Brain.*

When I first read the line—*"Your brain is for having ideas, not storing them"*—it felt like someone had opened a window in a dark room. I realized I had been using my mind as a warehouse, when it was meant to be a studio. My head was cluttered with storage, leaving little space for creation.

That was the day I decided: I will build a Second Brain.

Building My System

I began with small steps. Every idea, every note, every insight—I captured it. A single place, no matter if it was a line from a book, a spark for a film, or a half-formed concept for a startup.

Slowly, I organized it. I gave my ideas a home: projects for the now, areas for the ongoing, resources for the someday, archives for the past.

I distilled them, stripping away the noise until only the essence remained—the golden sentences, the distilled insights, the sparks that still glowed after the initial fire.

And then, I expressed. I turned notes into scripts, sketches into campaigns, whispers into strategies.

The Second Brain became not just storage, but a **factory of creation.**

I began to notice something subtle: my communication elevated. No longer scrambling for words or searching for scattered notes, I spoke with clarity. I wrote with weight. I built with momentum.

Peace began to replace the chaos. My mind, once frantic with keeping track, was now free—free to imagine, free to create, free to rest.

The Lesson of the Billionaire

In those moments, I thought of the stories of billionaires who transformed into philanthropists. At first, their empires were built on drive, ambition, relentless pursuit. But what allowed them to shift from *success to significance* was not just wealth—it was systems.

A billionaire cannot manage a fortune on memory alone. They build structures, teams, and frameworks to hold complexity. And when those systems run smoothly, a new horizon opens: the freedom to give back, to serve, to create impact beyond themselves.

In my own way, I felt the same shift. My Second Brain was my system. It held my thoughts, my work, my lessons. And because it carried the weight, I was free to dream larger, to think beyond myself, to align my skills not just with profit, but with purpose.

That is the quiet bridge between ambition and philanthropy: **systems that free the mind and spirit for higher callings**.

From Chaos to Contribution

I discovered that building a Second Brain wasn't just about productivity. It was about identity. It was about discovering how I learn, how I work, how I create—and then designing a life around that truth.

It gave me more than efficiency. It gave me satisfaction. It gave me peace.

And maybe this is what self-discovery really means. Not just finding out who you are, but also discovering *how to hold yourself together*—how to shape your creativity into something the world can touch.

When the mind is clear, creation becomes natural. And when creation flows, contribution follows. That is how one becomes not just a builder, but a giver.

And that is how a billionaire becomes a philanthropist.

Chapter 12

The Quiet Path of 80/20

I didn't stumble upon abundance by working harder than everyone else. I found it by working *differently*. The world celebrates the grind—the endless hustle of chasing more hours, more output, more recognition. But my breakthrough came when I slowed down and listened to a whisper of wisdom: **not everything matters equally.**

It was the 80/20 Principle that opened the door. Twenty percent of my efforts—just a sliver of my energy—were giving me nearly all my results. The rest? Noise. Distraction. Work that looked busy but didn't build anything lasting. When I finally saw that imbalance for what it was, I realized the true game wasn't about doing more; it was about doing less, better.

So, I started cutting. Ruthlessly, but quietly. I stopped scattering my time across the trivial many. I focused on the vital few—the projects, ideas, and practices that held real weight. Suddenly, I wasn't drained. I was alive.

That's when creativity surged. By freeing myself from the clutter, I had space to invent, to dream, to create something of my own. I built processes for myself—not rigid routines, but living systems that honored imagination. They took the 20% of sparks that mattered and grew them into flames. In that fire, I shaped the work that carried my fingerprint, not someone else's checklist.

What I discovered wasn't just productivity; it was peace. Calm settled in where stress had once lived. Satisfaction came not from completing endless tasks, but from nurturing the work that mattered most—the work that brought me joy. That alignment created an unexpected gift: abundance. Not the loud kind, but the quiet richness of having *enough* and then more than enough. Enough time to savor mornings. Enough energy to love people deeply. Enough resources to not only live well but to give well.

And so, I gave. The surplus of focus and wealth I cultivated through 80/20 thinking became fuel for philanthropy. I could invest in causes, in people, in futures larger than my own. Giving wasn't just an afterthought; it became my compass, turning my private success into shared prosperity.

Looking back, the math of my life became simple:

- **20% of effort** brought **80% of results.**
- **20% of creative processes** birthed **most of my originality.**
- **20% of choices** shaped **nearly all my happiness.**

The rest was clutter, and I left it behind.

Now, I live not as someone who conquered everything, but as someone who chose wisely. I chose to do less, but better. I chose to walk the quiet path of 80/20—and in that stillness, I found not just success, but freedom.

Chapter 13

Creativity Unlocked

The truth is, creativity doesn't thrive in chaos. It flourishes in space—quiet, uncluttered space where the mind is free to play. Before I discovered the 80/20 path, I tried to chase every idea. My notebooks were full, my mind was restless, but my results were thin. I was running after the trivial many, scattering my energy across too much.

Then came the shift. I realized not every idea deserved equal attention. Out of a hundred sparks, only a handful had the power to ignite a fire. I stopped hoarding every thought and started listening carefully for the few that stirred my spirit. Those ideas, the vital few, became my compass.

I built processes around them. Not rigid checklists, but creative systems that honored flow. I gave myself rituals that cleared distractions—early morning silence, walks that fed imagination, short bursts of deep focus. These weren't about discipline alone; they were about protection. Protection of the 20% of my ideas that mattered most.

What happened next felt like alchemy. The fog lifted. Instead of many unfinished sketches, I began finishing meaningful work. My creations carried soul because they came from a place of clarity. I wasn't trying to do everything—I was pouring myself into the few things that mattered. That concentration gave me a voice of my own.

Creativity became less of a chase and more of a dance. I had rhythm, calm, and space. I discovered that abundance in creativity wasn't about producing endless things, but about cultivating the rare gems and letting them shine.

Chapter 14

Wealth with Simplicity

Money is another mirror of imbalance. For years, I chased too many opportunities, spent in too many directions, and wondered why I felt stretched thin. Then the 80/20 lens revealed the truth: a small share of my investments generated most of my returns, and a small fraction of my spending drained most of my budget.

I made a decision. I would simplify. I cut the trivial expenses—the things that looked good in the moment but added nothing to the life I wanted. I honored the practice of saving first, setting aside a portion before I even thought of spending. I doubled down on the few investments that had proven resilient, the ones that quietly grew without drama.

It wasn't about hoarding or becoming frugal to the point of scarcity. It was about clarity. About focusing my financial energy on the vital few decisions that mattered most. With each step, a new kind of wealth emerged—not just numbers in an account, but the freedom to choose. Freedom to take risks on ideas I loved, freedom to say no to work that drained me, freedom to give generously without fear.

Wealth with simplicity wasn't about chasing everything. It was about choosing wisely, and then letting compounding—of money, of time, of trust—do its quiet work. That's how abundance found me: not by stretching, but by simplifying.

Chapter 15

Relationships that Matter

The 80/20 principle applies to the heart as much as it does to work and money. Not every relationship deserves equal weight. Some connections lifted me, inspired me, and brought joy far greater than their number. Others quietly drained me, asking much and giving little.

I realized I had been scattering my presence across too many people. So, I shifted. I chose presence with the ones who mattered most. I poured time into family, friends, and collaborators who carried depth. I gave them not just my hours but my attention. And the rest, I released gently, without resentment.

This was not about judgment but about alignment. Some relationships belong to certain seasons, and it is wise to let them go when their season has passed. By focusing on the vital few, my circle sharpened. It grew smaller, but it grew stronger. I had people I could lean on, celebrate with, dream with. And they had me.

The truth is, a life of quality relationships is worth infinitely more than a life of endless acquaintances. The richness of laughter shared, silence understood, and trust unspoken outweighs any crowd. In love and friendship, as in all things, the 80/20 path is clear: nurture the few, and let the many go.

Chapter 16

The Freedom of Giving

Abundance is never complete until it is shared. For me, the natural extension of the 80/20 path was philanthropy. I discovered that a small fraction of my contributions created the greatest ripple of change. Instead of spreading myself thin, I focused on causes where my energy, resources, and vision could multiply impact.

I chose deeply, not widely. I looked for people and projects where my presence made a real difference. Sometimes it was funding a dream. Sometimes it was mentorship. Sometimes it was building opportunities where none existed before. The principle was the same: focus on the vital few ways of giving that matter most.

Philanthropy gave me a new kind of freedom—the freedom to live for more than myself. Each act of giving pulled me further from the noise of personal success and closer to the melody of shared prosperity. I learned that when you give deeply, you don't diminish. You expand. The cycle of abundance grows wider, and life itself becomes richer.

Chapter 17

Living the 80/20 Way

The 80/20 principle is not just a strategy. It is a way of seeing the world. It whispers that less is more, that the vital few carry the weight of the whole, that wisdom lies in focus, not in frenzy.

Living the 80/20 way means choosing space over clutter, meaning over noise, depth over surface. It means investing in the handful of efforts, relationships, and causes that give life its shape. It means trusting that simplicity is not weakness, but strength.

My life, reimagined through 80/20, became a masterpiece of calm, satisfaction, and shared abundance. And it taught me a truth worth passing on: **when you choose the vital few and let the trivial many fall away, you don't just achieve more with less—you live more with less.**

ᢒ☆ᢒ

Chapter 18

Sow the Seeds of Today, for a New Life

I never rushed, yet he was never still. Every step he took between 2025 and 2027, and beyond, carried the weight of a man who knew he was walking into his own legend. Some saw him as just another dreamer. But he knew — dreamers drift. Builders endure.

The mornings were heavy with grind: emails unanswered, drafts half-broken, clients hard to convince. Nights bled into dawn with lines of code, character rigs, storyboards, and pitches that sometimes failed. Yet beneath the fatigue, there was always a hum — a sense that these struggles were not random. They were chiseling him, sharpening him, making him fit for something larger. His art was never just “design.” In his hands, pixels became breath, and technology bent toward storytelling. AR and VR weren’t gimmicks; they were portals. Characters he animated weren’t lifeless rigs; they carried soul, shadows, presence. Every project was both a deliverable and a declaration: *I am here. This is what I can do.*

But beyond the craft, destiny spoke. He could feel it in small wins that stacked into milestones: the freelance gigs that taught him grit, the first international project that affirmed his voice mattered beyond borders, the systems he built so his work wouldn’t just shine but scale.

By 2027, he wasn’t just “in the industry.” He *was* an industry in motion — a creator, a strategist, a storyteller whose name carried weight. Not because of fame, but because of consistency. He had sown his seeds — tiny decisions, brave pitches, relentless hours — and now the first shoots of his forest were breaking through the soil.

Those who crossed his path saw more than a man. They saw the rare fusion of fate and effort, the kind of person who makes you believe in possibility again. And him? He didn't boast. He simply kept moving, quietly planting, knowing the real harvest was still ahead.

Books poured from his mind like rivers carving valleys, each one a reflection of discovery, each one a torch lit for others to see. Millions of pages, millions of seeds, scattered into the world. He learned to prize every small thing — even a sip of coffee became a celebration, a reminder that life itself was the gift. And as his journey stretched wider, he grew into more than a creator; he became a giver, a philanthropist. His art had always carried heart, but now his life carried service.

There was always one story that stayed with him, a film that had etched itself into his soul — *The Pursuit of Happiness*. It reminded him of the simple truth that struggle is not the end but the forge. And in that forge, he shaped a life worth living.

The scene closes not with applause or accolades, but with something quieter. He stands by a window at dawn, a cup of coffee warming his hands. Outside, the first light brushes the skyline, turning shadows into shapes. In that silence, he smiles – not because he has arrived, but because he knows the journey is still alive, still unfolding. The seeds are planted, the forest is coming, and the horizon is infinite.

9 789358 985993

Printed at Repro India Ltd.